How To Build the ULTIMATE LinkedIn Profile In Under An Hour: Boost Your Branding, Attract Recruiters, And Find Your Next Job

Published by Andrew Macarthy

D0273619

Table Of Contents

Contents

Want to Find Your Next Job or Expand Your Business on LinkedIn? Why You Should Read This Book

In short, LinkedIn, with its 200 million+ members has fast become the tool of choice for a vast majority of employers and individuals seeking new workers and business opportunities. Depending on the recent studies you consult, up to 7 in every 10 employers is now using social networking to search for and vet potential candidates, and according to a CareerBuilder poll in 2012, that figure stands at a whopping 65 percent of recruiters researching on LinkedIn.

With its rising prominence online, a free LinkedIn profile is like an online business card, resume, and short sales pitch combined, and also provides you with a platform to interact and network with your peers.

Whether you are actively seeking a new job, just keeping your options open, or keen to connect with fellow professionals to improve your business prospects, the above statistics underscore the importance of creating and maintaining a thorough, accurate, and updated LinkedIn profile.

This book will teach you how you create a powerful LinkedIn profile in under an hour; one that will help you stand out from the vast majority of users on the site - some of whom might even be the competition for your next job - and impress your audience! Building a super optimized LinkedIn profile will keep people reading your profile for longer, get you noticed more in search, boost your professional image, and, with a little time spent managing your presence on the social network, help to open up a world of opportunity that has never been available to you before.

I wish you all the success in the world!

5 Ways To Write A Captivating LinkedIn Professional Headline And Make An Awesome First Impression

Robert Pratt

Digital Strategist specializing in Social Media, Local and Mobile Marketing

New York, New York | Marketing and Advertising

Previous   LiftEngine, e-Dialog, Acxiom Digital

Education   Indiana University - Kelley School of Business

Connect   Send InMail   500+ connections

Above :An example of a good LinkedIn Headline; Below: How a Headline appears in LinkedIn search.

Robert Pratt 2nd

Digital Strategist specializing in Social Media, Local and Mobile Marketing

Greater New York City Area · Marketing and Advertising

▸ 1 shared connection · Similar

Connect

Your LinkedIn Professional Headline - that's the few sentences of bold text (120 characters maximum to be exact) that sits below your name on your LinkedIn profile - is one of the site's most overlooked sections, but actually pretty crucial to increasing how "findable" and enticing you are to potential connections. And if one of your main aims with LinkedIn is to leverage the site for professional gain, then a well-crafted Headline is imperative.

By default, LinkedIn populates your headline with your current job title and employer, and that's how great swathes of people leave it - *bad move!* Your Headline sits in a prime position on your profile, and can be used to share your expertise, promote your core marketing message, and exude your personality. In order to get recruiters or potential connections to stop and pay attention, use your Headline to tell them **what you are, who you help, how you make their work/life better, and give proof that you are credible.** The way you craft your Headline depends on what your aims are, but here are five ways to do it well in a variety of situations:

Showcase your specialty.
With hundreds of millions of LinkedIn users, recruiters browsing LinkedIn are adept at breezing through hundreds of search results at a time, and if your Headline reads just something like *"Project Manager, Miami Marketing, Co."*, with nothing else about what you do, chances are they are going to skip right past it. A better example might read:

"Project manager who helps clients reach peak business performance. Former senior Project Manager for Ford Motor Co."

Speak directly to your audience
LinkedIn is a global stage for everything you have to offer a potential employer or connection, so speak to them directly in your Headline. For example, if you were an expert in helping grow startup businesses, you might write:

"Customer-focused pro who can take your new venture startup to the next level. Also run seminars, workshops, and training."

Be specific

If your LinkedIn Headline told a recruiter you were a psychologist in California, what would really help to make you stand it out if you were even more specific. Remember, there will be thousands of profiles with bland and generic Headlines, so give yours the best chance of standing out. An example along the psychologist lines might read:

"Education-specialized psychologist;15 yrs helping kids overcome learning troubles and develop socio-emotional abilities."

Include relevant keywords, but don't cram

As well as crafting an appealing Headline, it is also important to consider keywords. Think about the kind of search terms the people you appeal to or want t connect with will be using to find you when recruiting via LinkedIn. Don't pile them into your Headline and damage its readability or flow, but do try to feature a couple of the keywords most important to who you are and what you can offer. An example might read:

"Executive Recruiter who helps Fortune 500 companies find top tech talent. Clients include Microsoft and Apple."

Be creative, not generic

Writing a creative LinkedIn Headline can be a great way of boosting your personal brand and catching the attention of recruiters and connections, but for the love of all that is holy, avoid empty buzzwords and phrases like *"outside-of-*

the-box thinker, " "problem-solver" or "strategic planner".
These clichés mean nothing without context. At best they
are cheesy, and at worst they will turn away many more
people than they attract.

How to change your LinkedIn Headline

1. Hover your cursor over "Profile" at the top of your
homepage and select "Edit Profile."
2. Click the blue pencil icon to the left of your current
professional headline, below your name at the top of the
profile.
3. Type in your changes.
4. Click "Save."
5. Click "Done editing."

How to Choose The Right Profile Photo to Capture Your Intended Audience, And Optimize It to Be Found In Search

Above: Three examples of great LinkedIn profile photos.

The inherent social nature of LinkedIn means that people *want* to connect with others - including you. In a lot of cases, a big part of instigating this interaction is if you have a great profile photo. In fact, according to LinkedIn, adding a profile photo makes your profile 7x more likely to be found in searches, so it is well worth taking the time and effort to get a nice one taken! If you don't have a profile photo, then your profile will look generic in LinkedIn search results, and is *much* more likely to be skipped over by potential recruiters and prospects.

As well as having a profile photo in the first place, the type of photo you upload is also crucial. The best LinkedIn profile photos are professionally-taken headshots, with the person looking smart and smiling in front of a light background. A cheaper (but no less effective) option is to have a family member or friend take a similar photo of you whilst outdoors on a bright and sunny day.

LinkedIn profile photos display at a size of 200 x 200 pixels, so yours should ideally be a square of a larger size - 500 x 500 pixels is the maximum - so that it will look crisp when it is scaled down, otherwise you'll be left with a tiny photo and a big grey border. When you save your photo ready for upload, don't just name it *me.png or profilepic.png*. Instead, for a subtle search engine optimization boost, call it something like *your-name-job-title-location.png*.

Note: If you work in an industry that does not require you to dress up in a suit and tie or other smart outfit for work, you may want to choose a more casual profile photo to reflect you and your personality. Whatever you choose, remember the golden rules: up close, smiling, and light background!

Current Photo	Upload a Photo
	You can upload a JPG, GIF or PNG file (File size limit is 4 MB).

Current Photo

Upload a Photo

You can upload a JPG, GIF or PNG file (File size limit is 4 MB).

Choose File   No file chosen

Upload Photo   or Cancel

By clicking "Upload Photo", you certify that you have the right to distribute this photo and that it

Edit Photo
Delete Photo

In addition to users I message, my profile photo is visible to...

◉ My Connections
◯ My Network
◯ Everyone

Save Settings

Above: Uploading a LinkedIn profile photo.

How to add or edit your LinkedIn profile photo

1. If you have not yet added a LinkedIn profile photo, click "Edit Profile" on your profile page and then click the placeholder image on your profile. Otherwise, click the camera icon on top of your current picture.

2. Click "Choose File" to find the photo you wish to use.

3. Click "Upload Photo". You can upload JPG, GIF or PNG files.

Note: If your photo is not a square, click the "Edit Photo" link and drag and resize the yellow outline to highlight the portion that you want to appear in your profile image. Click "Save Photo."

4. Select who you want the photo to be visible to: My Connections, M Network, or Everyone (recommended).

5. Click Save Settings.

9 Secrets to Writing A Compelling LinkedIn Summary

Above: An example of a great LinkedIn Summary.

On a site where millions of people are vying for attention, first impressions count. And after your Headline and profile photo, your LinkedIn Summary is the first detailed opportunity you have to impress a potential employer or contact. It's also the only area on the profile where you get to define yourself from scratch, uninhibited by dates, labels or other text boxes. What you choose to write in this section can make the difference between professional success or a sorry state of affairs for your personal LinkedIn account.

 Note: Never leave the Summary section blank! A missing Summary means that the first thing a viewer of your profile sees is your Experience section. Your profile will be left looking like a resume without a summary statement at the top, or a written essay without an introductory paragraph.

Set your goals

Before you write your LinkedIn Summary, be clear in your mind about why you are using LinkedIn. Are you seeking a job? Contentedly employed, but want to build up your personal brand? Looking to strengthen your professional network? Hoping to land new customers for your business? The likelihood is that you have several goals.

The vast majority of LinkedIn users haven't given any thought to who they are trying to impress or why they are using LinkedIn, which leaves them with summaries that are unclear and lack direction. Don't let this be you!

Write in the first person

Writing a Summary about yourself in the 3rd person is a theatrical gimmick that doesn't, no matter what anyone says, make you come across as revered, important, and someone that commands respect in your field. In fact, it's more likely to make you seem pompous, out of touch and pretentious. First person is the way forward!

One good way to start is to include your full name in the first sentence of your Summary, e.g., *'My name is Mark Jones, and....'* because your name is a keyword and this sentence also sets the stage for everything you're about to say too.

Expand on the problems you solve

Whatever your aims on LinkedIn, your Summary should expand on the Headline you create by telling readers which business-related problems you can solve. Again - and in more detail - tell people who you help and how you can help them if they choose to connect.

Prove your credibility
It is safe to assume that the people (particularly recruiters) who read profiles on LinkedIn will be - rightly or wrongly - skeptical about every word you write. Anyone can reel off a series of amazing career achievements in flowery prose in an attempt to impress, so it is important that you differentiate yourself by highlighting several quantifiable and relevant achievements as evidence of your value.

Tell a story
In an era where the job market is more competitive than ever, it is not enough to simply let your experience speak for itself. You need to be your own brand ambassador and ensure that your professional online prospectus is unique, engaging and well written. If you can show readers of your LinkedIn profile that you have a compelling story to back up your chosen career path (and the obstacles you have overcome on the way), or a sincere reason why you might want to be seeking a new job in a different field, you have a better chance of appealing to their human side, and twigging their emotions. This is something all the best LinkedIn profiles do very well. In essence, if you can grab someone's attention with something about yourself that they wouldn't know from your ordinary résumé details, you're heading in the right direction.

Include contact information
One of the main reasons people use LinkedIn is to connect with others, so make sure you include your contact information - your e-mail address as a minimum - in your summary. The risk of being targeted by spammers is far

outweighed by the potential benefit of being contacted by an interested party, especially if you are putting yourself out there as you look for new job opportunities. If you are very concerned about spam, set up a new e-mail address specifically for displaying on LinkedIn. Don't forget to check it often!

Include a CTA, invite users to connect!

Studies of the psychology of marketing show that simply asking people what you want them to do can greatly increase conversion rates. In the case of LinkedIn, a successful conversion involves being contacted by a recruiter or other prospect. As the site's search feature is extremely connection-driven, a wise move is to include a call-to-action (CTA) at the end of your Summary section, encouraging people to connect with you.

Keep it brief

As you are probably all too aware from the way you live your own life, we are all very busy. On the Internet, the majority of people skim-read instead of giving onscreen words their full attention, especially a LinkedIn recruiter sifting through reams of profiles. To this end, while the Summary box on LinkedIn offers you 2,000 characters to fill, using up every inch of space probably isn't the wisest idea, no matter the keyword benefits.

Imagine someone had just 10 seconds to read your Summary - a lot of the time that's all it'll get in the real world anyway - and think about what you would write to grab their attention. Are your thoughts interesting and original? Congratulations, you may have just bought yourself another small chunk of a readers' time.

Avoid clichéd buzzwords
When you're putting together your LinkedIn Summary, it is, as you know, important to stand out from the crowd. The worst thing you can do is make your write-up sound like everyone else's. One big part of making this happen - as you will do in your Headline - is to avoid the use of so-called buzzwords, terms that have sprung up in use in professional circles over the years. While at one time they might have stood for something, now they are just embarrassing! Here are the top 10 terms that are overused by professionals based in the United States, courtesy of LinkedIn:

- Extensive experience
- Innovative
- Motivated
- Results-oriented
- Dynamic
- Proven track record
- Team player
- Fast-paced
- Problem solver
- Entrepreneurial

7 Ways to Optimize Your LinkedIn Experience Section For Maximum Impact and Exposure

LinkedIn states that having your two most recent positions listed in the Experience section of your profile makes it 12x more likely to be found in search. With that in mind, here are plenty of ways to make sure your Experience section on LinkedIn stands head and shoulders above the competition:

Craft descriptive titles, include keywords for SEO

Each job position in your Experience section gives you a maximum of 100 characters to describe your role and, like the Headline section of your LinkedIn profile, this is fertile ground for placing relevant keywords to boost your SEO on the site. For example, a job title that might ordinarily read *"IT Trainer and Consultant"* can easily be transformed into something much more powerful like *"CEO | IT Trainer and Technology Consultant (Specializing in MS Office Suite)."* See how much more descriptive and appealing it is? The extra keywords give it a welcome boost too!

Add detail, don't just list

The first thing to note about your Experience section is that you should not just treat it as a simple list of the jobs you have done, where you were based, and the years you spent in the position. Remember to describe your job duties in a fair amount of detail, and in a way that will add interest and credibility to you, your story, and your personal brand.

Talk about your achievements, give specifics

For each position in your Experience section, include details that show readers why you are/were good at your job. Be sure to include bulleted accomplishments that demonstrate your diverse experience, your professionalism, and your ability to get important stuff done. If you are able to be specific with statistics and /or results, that's even better.

Note: See the *"How to Make Your Profile Eye-Catching In LinkedIn Search With Bullet Points, Stars, and Other Special Character"* chapter for tips on adding bullet points to your Experience section and others.

Highlight customers served and include a testimonial

One of the most powerful ways of connecting with a reader of your profile is to hammer home the big difference you make to the people you help in your current role, or those that you have helped in the past. One of the easiest ways to do this is to lift a short testimonial from the Recommendations section of your LinkedIn profile (covered in a future chapter), or from your own website or blog. Don't forget to credit the testimonial with the customer's name, their company, and the position they hold there.

Mention promotions

Whichever tier of importance you are currently at or finished up at in a previous job, it's always a good idea to mention in your Experience section, where relevant, promotions you earned, in order to let recruiters and other readers of your profile know how you got there. Imagine how much more of an impression you will make if you talk about how you started off on the bottom rung on the ladder and slowly but surely (or quickly!) rose to command a much more senior role at your places of work, rather than making it sound like you waltzed right for no real reason.

Tie the past to the present
Help readers of your LinkedIn profile understand how your past experience makes you a better fit for the role you want, or the people you want to connect with, today. Do this by highlighting characteristics, traits, and results from your previous jobs that most closely align to your current situation.

Re-order current roles by importance
While LinkedIn encourages to you have all of your experience in chronological order (and you *cannot* re-order past positions), you may want to re-order current positions to group the most relevant information, so to keep your intended audience interested and engaged. Here's how:

1. Move your cursor over Profile at the top of your homepage and select "Edit Profile."
2. Click the arrow icon next to the title of the position you want to move and drag it to a spot above or below another current position.

How to Populate Additional LinkedIn Sections And How to Re-Order All Sections By Importance

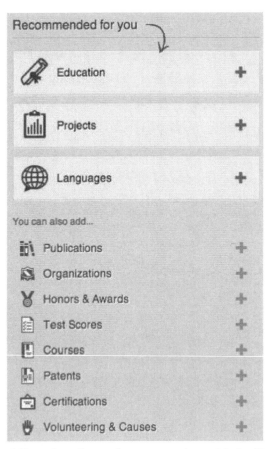

Above: Adding details to the more minor LinkedIn sections.

While the sections of your LinkedIn profile we have already covered are the most important in terms of getting you noticed, there are several smaller sections that LinkedIn encourages you to populate - and I do too. Any sections you haven't taken advantage of yet will show up on the right side of your screen when you go to edit your profile. They include a place to show off:

- Your Publications
- Your Education
- Your Projects
- Languages you speak
- Organizations you belong to
- Honors & Awards you have received
- Test Scores
- Courses you've taken
- Patents you own
- Certifications you've been awarded
- Volunteering & Causes you have been involved in

It doesn't take long to do, but you can be sure that many potential recruiters or connections will appreciate the effort.

How to re-order sections of your LinkedIn profile

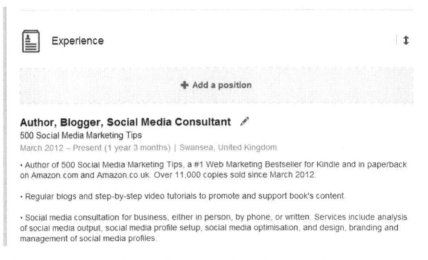

Above: Re-arranging LinkedIn sections by dragging the arrow icon.

LinkedIn allows you to re-order the sections of your profile and decide which sections are most important to you, and the ones you want visitors to your profile to see first - your education, your work experience, your recommendations, or anything else. To start re-arranging, click on the "Edit Profile" button and look for the draggable handles on each section. Simply click and drag each section up or down until they are in your preferred order.

How to Add Skills & Expertise to Your LinkedIn Profile, And How to Find the Best Ones to List

Å   Skills & Expertise

Most endorsed for...

99+	Medical Coding	
72	Revenue Cycle	
72	Health Information...	
70	Healthcare	
69	HIPAA	
56	EHR	
29	EMR	
28	Healthcare Consulting	
25	Healthcare Information...	
20	Medicaid	

Todd also knows about...

19 Healthcare Management	19 Medical Billing	17 Hospitals	16 ICD-9
13 ICD-10	13 Medical Records	12 Medical Terminology	11 CPT
9 Temporary Placement	9 Medicare	8 HCPCS	7 Coders
7 Revenue Cycle Management	5 Training	4 Medical Compliance	See 5+ ›

Above: An example of a well populated and endorsed Skills & Expertise section

LinkedIn allows users to list up to 50 Skills & Expertise on their profile. Maintaining a relevant list of skills and expertise will help others understand your strengths and encourage recruiters to match you with the right opportunities available for you.

How to add Skills & Expertise

1. Move your cursor over Profile at the top of your home page and select "Edit Profile."
2. Scroll down to the Skills & Expertise section and click the pencil icon in the upper right.
3. Type the name of a skill and then choose it from the drop-down list that appears. If your skill doesn't appear, type in the skill name manually and in full.
4. Click Add.
5. Click Save.

Above: Using the Skills and Expertise page for inspiration.

Need inspiration? Use the Skills and Expertise page

If you aren't sure what skills to add to your profile, you can visit the Skills & Expertise page (http://www.linkedin.com/skills/your_skills?trk=skill_page) for help. Suggested skills and expertise will be displayed based on the details you have included in your profile. Inspired? Click "Add" next to any of these skills or click the "Find and Edit" link and just start typing in some of your own.

How to Encourage Endorsements to Showcase Your Skills and Expertise

An Endorsement is a one-click way for your connections to give their backing to the Skills & Expertise listed on your LinkedIn profile. Skill endorsements are a simple and effective way of building your professional brand and engaging your network via your LinkedIn profile. Skills with the most endorsements will be listed first, while those without endorsements are displayed according to when they were added. Accumulating a high number of endorsements for a skill adds credibility to your profile, and shows that your professional network recognizes you have that skill.

Receiving Endorsements
Your connections can endorse you for a skill or expertise - even one you haven't listed on your profile. You'll see these skills in a blue box at the top of your profile. Click the X next to any you don't want to add, then click "Add to Profile" to add the listed skills to your profile. These items won't be visible to others until you choose to add them to your profile.

Note: You don't need to ask for a skill endorsement to receive one. You'll also be notified by email when you receive an endorsement.

Encouraging Endorsements

One of the best ways to encourage endorsements is to endorse others. Once they are notified of their endorsements from you, with any luck, they will return the favor. Before you endorse your connections, though, make sure the skills and expertise you most want to be endorsed for are ready and waiting on your profile to be clicked.

Hide Or Unhide Endorsements

You can choose to hide or unhide your skill endorsements if you wish. Here's how:

1. Click "Edit Profile" in the top section of your profile.
2. Scroll down to the Skills & Expertise section and click the blue pencil icon.
3. Click the "Manage Endorsements" link.
4. Use the scroll bar on the left side of the box to view your list of skills.
5. Click on a skill to reveal the connections who've endorsed you for that skill.
6. Uncheck the box next to any people whose endorsements you want to hide. Or, check the box next to any you want to unhide.

Hide All Endorsements By Default

You also have the option to keep all of your skill endorsements hidden by default:

1. Click "Edit Profile" in the top section of your profile.
2. Scroll down to the Skills & Expertise section and click the blue pencil icon.
3. Click the green check mark next to Display your endorsements?
4. Select No, do not show my endorsements from the dropdown list.

5. Click Save.

Note: You may check or uncheck the box next to show/hide all endorsements to take action on all endorsements under one skill at once.

How to Edit Your Contact Info and Customize the Website Text Links to Your Blog, Website, Portfolio, etc.

Above: A Contact Info section with customized website links.

In your LinkedIn profile's "Contact Info" section (click on the grey "Contact Info" box near the top of your profile to expand it), your Email address, IM, Phone number and address will visible to your connections. This is fairly useful in itself, but even better is that your Twitter handle and Websites are visible to *everyone* on LinkedIn, and this is where you can really take advantage. First, the basics....

How to add or edit information in your Contact Info section

1. Click "Profile" at the top of your LinkedIn homepage.
2. Click "Edit" located in the top section of your profile.
3. Click "Edit Contact Info" located in this same section. The section will expand.
4. Click the pencil icon next to the section you'd like to edit, then make and confirm your changes.

5. When you're done, click "Save.

Above: Creating custom website links on yourLinkedIn profile

How to customize text links to external websites

Here's the sneaky bit... notice that the drop-down menu for Websites gives you choices like "Personal Website," "Company Website," and "Blog"? When you choose these, the text link that displays in your "Contact Info" section is exactly the same - functional, but very generic.

Instead, choose the "Other..." option from the Websites drop-down menu. When you do this, an extra text box will appear allowing you to enter a custom Website Title, and now *this* will be the text link that appears on your profile. So instead of something nonspecific "Blog" or "Personal Website," you can insert much more appealing names or even call-to-actions, like "Hire Me" or "My Portfolio."

It's a small detail that, you never know, could make all the difference in attracting someone to get in touch with a new opportunity!

How to Choose A Custom LinkedIn URL, e.g linkedin.com/yourname

Customize your public profile URL   ✕

Enhance your personal brand by creating a custom URL for your LinkedIn public profile.

If you change your URL, your current custom URL will no longer be valid.

uk.linkedin.com/in/ | andrewmacarthy

Note: Your custom URL must contain 5 - 30 letters or numbers. Please do not use spaces, symbols, or special characters.

[Set Custom URL] or Cancel

Above: Editing a custom LinkedIn URL.

One way to easily enhance your personal brand is by creating a custom URL for your LinkedIn public profile. By default, the URL to your profile will be a mixture of your name, hyphens, and numbers, something like: *www.linkedin.com/pub/your-name/6/8b2/31b* Hardly rolls of the tongue, does it?

LinkedIn allows you to change and simplify your profile's default URL to become something more memorable like *www.linkedin.com/yourname*, This update will allow you to promote and share your the URL LinkedIn presence a lot more effectively.

How to choose a custom LinkedIn URL

1. Move your cursor over your name in the top right of your homepage and select "Settings."
2. Click the "Edit your public profile" link near the bottom right of the next page.
3. In the Your public profile URL box on the right, click the "Customize your public profile URL" link.
4. Type the last part of your new custom URL in the text box.
5. Click "Set Custom URL."

Note: Your custom URL must contain 5 - 30 letters or numbers. Do not use spaces, symbols, or special characters, as these will not be accepted.

Please also note that some URLs may be unavailable. If a LinkedIn member uses a URL and then changes it, the URL they first chose will be unavailable for use by another member for several months. This gives the person a chance to reclaim it in case they change their mind. LinkedIn is unable to make these URLs available upon request. If the URL you want isn't available, you will need to select a different one.

How to Add Interactive Media Samples to Your Profile: Show Off Your Work and WOW Prospects

Above: An example of media samples displayed on a LinkedIn profile.

In the spring of 2013, LinkedIn began rolling out a feature that allows users to show samples of their work on their profile, in the Summary, Education, and Experience sections. In its own words, this means you can *"illustrate your greatest achievements in the form of stunning images, compelling videos, innovative presentations and more,"* for all to see. For a social network that has been text-heavy for so many years, this is huge! As well as improving the aesthetics of your profile with bursts of color, media samples also mean potential connections and recuiters can learn more about you and admire examples of your work without even leaving the site.

There are about tons of different ways that you can use visual profile elements to market yourself on LinkedIn. Here are just a few:

- Speakers can link to their presentations on Slideshare or clips from YouTube.
- Graphic & web designers can link to Behance to highlight their portfolio.
- People who help businesses build traffic for websites can link to Quantcast profiles to show off the sites they have helped.
- Entrepreneurs can link to their Kickstarter project to encourage donations for their latest start up idea.
- Podcasters can link to their latest and best shows.
- Photographers can link to a portfolio of their images on Pinterest.
- Authors can link to documents with samples of their work.

Sounds good, no? Here's how to add them...

How to add media samples to your Linkedin profile:
1. Hover your cursor over "Profile" at the top of your homepage and select "Edit Profile."
2. Scroll down to the section you want to add a sample to and hover your cursor over the add media icon (looks like a square with a plus sign). **Note:** If you don't see the add media icon you don't have access to this feature yet.

3. Select "Upload File" if you'd like to display the media sample on your profile *or* select "Add Link" if you want to link to content that exists on another website instead.

If you chose to add a link, type or paste the link to your content into the "Add a link" field.
If you chose to upload a file, select the file from your desktop. A picture of your content will display with pre-filled Title and Description fields.

Note: This process may take several seconds. You must use a compatible file type or content provider for best results. You can edit the content in uploaded files.

4. Click Save. An update may go out on the homepages of your network, letting others know you added the media file or link.

How to edit the title and description fields of your media samples.
1. Hover your cursor over "Profile" at the top of your homepage and select "Edit Profile."
2. Scroll down to the media sample you want to edit and click the pencil icon in the lower right corner.
3. Click inside the Title and Description fields to edit the text. When you're done, click "Save."

Note: The media sample's image and its link cannot be edited, and if you choose to link to content from an unsupported provider, you won't be able to add a description. The media may also not display when clicked on. Instead, a "Show Original" button will display, taking the viewer to the content on the original website when clicked.

How to move media samples from one section to another

1. Hover your cursor over "Profile" at the top of your homepage and select "Edit Profile."
2. Scroll down to the sample you'd like to move and click the pencil icon in its lower right corner.
3. Click the dropdown menu under "Move this media to" and choose which section of your profile you'd like to move it to. When you're done. click "Save."

Note: To rearrange items within the same section of your profile, click "Edit" on your profile and drag the items to rearrange them in the order you desire.

How to remove a media sample from your profile:

1. Hover your cursor over "Profile" at the top of your homepage and select "Edit Profile."
2. Scroll down to the sample you'd like to remove and click the pencil icon in its lower right corner.
3. Click "Remove this Media" and then click "Yes" to remove it.

How to Promote Your LinkedIn Profile Online and Offline: Widgets, E-mail Signatures, and Real World Marketing

There are several ways that you can use to promote your LinkedIn profile, both online and in the real world. By making people aware of your of your profile - in simple, subtle, and effective ways - you increase the number of eyeballs viewing a page where they can see who you are, and find everything they need to know about you in a professional capacity. Hopefully this will lead to more connections and job opportunities coming your way.

Share your custom URL by word of mouth and on other online profile
By following the steps in an earlier chapter, you should now have a nice and neat custom URL for your LinkedIn profile. Not only is this easy for people to remember in person - word-of-mouth marketing, especially if it is just www.linkedin.com/yourname, but it can also be placed where many people are likely to see it, such as on business cards, in the "About" section of your Facebook profile, the background design of your Twitter profile and on your blog or website.

Promote your profile by adding a badge to your blog, online resume, or website:

Choose a button:	... then copy and paste the code (includes a link to your public profile):
View my profile on Linked[in] See how we're connected	**TypePad Users** Click here to add this button to your TypePad blog: Add to My TypePad Blog
View my profile on Linked [in] (160x33)	```<a href="http://uk.linkedin.com/in/andrewmacarthy"> <img src="http://www.linkedin.com/img/webpromo/btn_viewmy_160x33.png" width="160" height="33" border="0" alt="View Andrew Macarthy's profile on```
my Linked [in] profile (160x33)	```<a href="http://uk.linkedin.com/in/andrewmacarthy"> <img src="http://www.linkedin.com/img/webpromo/btn_myprofile_160x33.png" width="160" height="33" border="0" alt="View Andrew Macarthy's profile on```

AbAbove: Creating a LinkedIn profile button for a website or blog.

Embed a LinkedIn "View My Profile" button to your online resume, blog, or website

Another good way to promote your LinkedIn profile is by adding a visual badge to your blog, online resume, or website:

1. Visit http://www.linkedin.com/profile/profile-badges
2. Decide on the button you'd like to use, then copy and paste the adjacent HTML code onto your site.

Note: The badge you embed will automatically include a link to your LinkedIn profile.

Create an email signature that contains your public profile URL

You can also create and edit your LinkedIn email signature from the Create Email Signature page.

Above: An example of a LinkedUn email signature.

1. Visit http://www.linkedin.com/signature?display=
You can also find the page required by clicking the "Tools"
link at the bottom of your LinkedIn profile and clicking
"Try It Now" next to the "Email Signature" option.
2. Click the "view gallery" link or choose a design from the
"Select Layout" section.
3. Add to or edit any fields.
4. Scroll to the bottom and click the link at that says, "Click
here for instructions".
5. Copy the code created, choose your email client from the
drop-down menu and follow those instructions to add the
signature.

How to Make Your LinkedIn Profile Visible And Appealing to Non-Members: Customize How Your Public Profile Appears in Search

Customize Your Public Profile

Control how you appear when people search for you on Google, Yahoo!, Bing, etc.

Profile Content

○ Make my public profile visible to **no one**

◉ Make my public profile visible to **everyone**

☑ Basics
Name, industry, location, number of recommendations

☐ Picture

☐ Headline

☐ Summary

☐ Current Positions

☐ Past Positions

☐ Publications

☐ Skills

☐ Education

☐ Additional Information

☐ Interested In...

Above: The box used to customize your public LinkedIn profile.

While those who become part of your LinkedIn network (i.e. your direct connections) will be able to see your LinkedIn profile in full when logged into the site, you have considerable control over what portions of your profile are displayed to the public - those not signed in, and those who are not members of LinkedIn.

This privacy control is important because, in a search for your name, LinkedIn profiles can rank highly in Google and other search engines. Many more people than you might think could find your LinkedIn profile and find a way to connect with you from the sections of your profile you choose to show, even if they don't belong to LinkedIn.

LinkedIn makes it really easy to control how your public profile appears when people search for you on Google, Yahoo!, Bing, etc. Here's how to manage what is seen and what remains hidden:

How to edit what's visible to the public
1. Login to LinkedIn, hover over the "Profile" link in the main menu bar at the top of the page and select "Edit Profile".

2. Click "Edit" next to your LinkedIn profile URL, which sits below your profile photo. The Public Profile page will open.

3. On the right-hand side of the page, you will see the "Customize Your Public Profile" box. To disallow the public from seeing any part of your LinkedIn profile (not recommended), click the button next to "Make my public profile visible to no one..."

4. ...Otherwise, click the button next to "Make my public profile visible to everyone," If you choose this option, your profile Basics - Name, Industry, Location, and number of recommendations - will be selected by default as the minimum you are allowed to show. Then, check as many more boxes as you like to tell LinkedIn what sections (and sub-sections) of your profile you want to be visible to the public, including Picture, Headline, Current Positions, and Education.

5. That's it, your changes will be saved automatically as you go.

How to Make Your Profile Eye-Catching In LinkedIn Search With Bullet Points, Stars, and Other Special Characters

Above: A LinkedIn Headline with custom unicode to add stars as bullets

Have you ever noticed special characters in someone's LinkedIn profile or other social media update - bullet points, stars, check marks, hearts and the like - and wondered how they got there? The characters are "unicode" - a universally recognized system for handling and displaying text - and are meant to be able to be viewed on almost any platform.

Many people put special characters - bullet points and stars are the two most common types - in their Headline so that it stands out amongst other profiles within LinkedIn search. As recruiters scan hundreds of profiles at a time, a smattering of unicode can be a subtle, but effective way of getting your profile noticed.

Unicode text can also be used in different sections of your LinkedIn profile - specifically your Summary and Experience. Using unicode to create bullet points in these sections can make potentially a lot of text much more readable.

How to insert unicode characters into your LinkedIn Profile

Each piece of unicode is represented by a short combination of letters and symbols. When pasted into your LinkedIn profile and saved, they will magically transform into the bullet, star, heart, etc, you want people to see. Here's an example of how to add unicode bullet points to your Experience section:

1. Find the code for unicode bullet points. There is a full list of unicode here: http://en.wikipedia.org/wiki/Unicode The code we want is •
2. On your LinkedIn profile, click "Edit Profile" at the top, scroll down and click the blue arrow icon next to the job position you want to add bullet points to.
3. Place your cursor at the beginning of the first line where you want to add a bullet, and paste in the unicode. Press the space bar once to add a gap between the bullet point and the text it sits next to. Repeat this step for as many lines as you wish to add bullets to.
4. Click "Save".

And voila, you now have bullet points in your profile text. If you ever return to edit a section that you have added bullets to, the • unicode will not be visible; it is replaced with a single space at the beginning of a line. To remove the bullet, delete this space and click "Save."

 Experience

Author, Blogger, Social Media Consultant
500 Social Media Marketing Tips
March 2012 – Present (1 year 3 months) | Swansea, United Kingdom

• Author of 500 Social Media Marketing Tips, a #1 Web Marketing Bestseller for Kindle and in paperback on Amazon.com and Amazon.co.uk. Over 11,000 copies sold since March 2012.

• Regular blogs and step-by-step video tutorials to promote and support book's content.

• Social media consultation for business, either in person, by phone, or written. Services include analysis of social media output, social media profile setup, social media optimisation, and design, branding and management of social media profiles.

Above: A subtle use of unicode to make add bullet points to a LinkedIn profile.

A word of warning: even unicode characters don't always display properly, so always test one or two first before going the whole hog throughout your profile. If you've already seen a particular unicode symbol working on a different LinkedIn profile, chances it will be fine on yours too.

The one last thing to consider is that special characters - especially if they're stars, circles, smiley faces, etc. - are not considered by everyone to be business-like, and that they do not deserve a place on anyone's LinkedIn profile. In general, don't go too wild, but it all depends on your career path and the people viewing you that you think the code might or might not resonate with. For example, stars might work better on the profile of an entertainer than they would on a lawyer!

Three Quick And Easy Ways to Start to Grow Your LinkedIn Network

Once you have set up and optimized your LinkedIn profile, you will want to start building your network - and thus, the number of people who can easily check you out - by making connections.

You can ask someone to join your LinkedIn network by sending them an invitation to connect. If they accept your invitation, they become a 1st-degree connection. LinkedIn recommends that you only send invitations to people you know well and/or trust as 1st-degree connections are given access to view your whole profile, not just the bits you choose to display publically. By the way, second degree connections are those people who are connected to people you are connected to, and third degree connections are connections of those second degree connections.

LinkedIn encourages you to only connect with people you really know, and they reserve the right to **suspend your ability to connect with people if you keep sending invitations to people who consequently flag you as someone they do not know** - the limit is five times of them being notified that this this happening. If your account is restricted, you will then need enter a person's email address if you ask them to connect with you until such a time that the ban is lifted. In order words, be careful about who you send invitations to!

Note: The following methods are a good way to give your number of connections an initial boost, but I wouldn't recommend using them other than for finding your closest colleagues or friends for the reasons above and those given in the *"How to Craft Killer Connection Invitations in Three Simple Steps"* chapter of this book, as they only allow you to send cookie-cutter invites.

See who you already know on LinkedIn

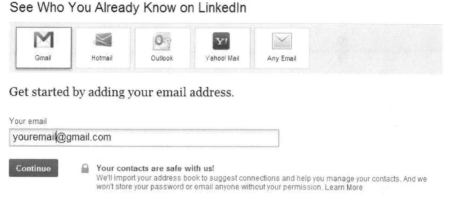

Above: Using e-mail contacts to find existing LinkedIn members to connect with.

1. Hover over the Contact link at the top of the site and click "Add Connections," then you will be asked to select your e-mail client - Gmail, Hotmail, Outlook, Yahoo! Mail or Other, and to enter your e-mail address.

On the page, click "Continue" and LinkedIn will lift all of the contacts from your e-mail address book who are already on the site. Check the people you would like to connect with, and click "Add Connections." Lastly, choose anyone who isn't on LinkedIn to join and connect with you and click "Add to Network."

Connect with colleagues
Visit http://www.linkedin.com/people/reconnect?posId=0 and you will see a page that lists the companies you have included as your places of employment on LinkedIn, and all of the people that work at said companies. Choose the people you want to connect with, and send them personal invitations using the method detailed in the next chapter of this book.

Alumni connections
Click the Alumni tab seen on the previous page, and you will be able to see and connect with people you may know from the schools you have added to your LinkedIn profile.

How to Use Activity Updates and LinkedIn Signal to Spread Your Name and Expertise to Connections and the Wider LinkedIn Community

If you are familiar with posting status updates on sites like Facebook and Twitter and monitoring your friends' posts , you may have noticed that LinkedIn offers something very similar - the Activity feed. This, along with the status box is your chance to let people in your network - and the wider LinkedIn community - know about what you are up to in your professional life, any great content you have created (blogs, infographics, videos, etc.), or useful resources that you want to share.

By posting updates regularly - at least once a day is a good target to aim for, but a couple of times is ideal - your updates will appear on the home pages of all your connections (unless they have turned this function off), as well as in LinkedIn Signal: (accessed via the "Signal" sub-menu from the "News" option on your LinkedIn home page or at http://www.linkedin.com/signal/). Signal lets you see and filter updates from LinkedIn professionals who choose to make their updates visible to anyone. Signal allows LinkedIn users to:

- Browse real-time updates with content summaries and direct links to the full content.
- Filter updates to show only those that you care about.
- Search for keywords, topics, companies or people across the updates stream.
- Save your search and check for updates later.
- Find trending links and Industry top headlines.

With these bullet points mind, just think how posting regularly could benefit your mission to "advertise" yourself to recruiters and other professionals on LinkedIn. You can also comment on and share other people's updates in Signal, and it's well worth doing that to dot your name around the site and help build relationships too.

How to post LinkedIn updates and set sharing options

1. Place your cursor in the Activity feed, available either from your LinkedIn home page or at the top of your profile.
2. Type an update. You can include links if you wish.
3. Choose who you want to share the update with via the "Share with" drop-down menu. Select from just your connections, the whole of LinkedIn, or LinkedIn + Twitter (recommended).

Note: LinkedIn also allows you to mention other users or companies in your status updates by preceding their name with an @ symbol, and to group similar types of content together with #hashtags. Hashtags are always a good idea, and you should think up of one or two (any more gets annoying or distracting for others) to accompany your activity updates, e.g. #marketing #socialmedia.

The LinkedIn Sharing Bookmarklet

It's well worth installing LinkedIn's Sharing Bookmarklet, which allows you to share anything from your web browser straight into your LinkedIn Activity feed.

Easily Share From Anywhere

Share webpages with your professional network and groups straight from your browser even when you're not on LinkedIn

Drag button above to browser toolbar to install

Above: Installing the "Share on LinkedIn" bookmarklet.

How to install the Sharing Bookmarklet

1. Click on the "Tools" link at the bottom of your LinkedIn home page, then click the "Sharing Bookmarklet" tab at the top of the next page.

2. LinkedIn's browser of choice for the Sharing Bookmarklet is Google Chrome. If this is your browser, simply click on and drag the "Share on LinkedIn" button to your bookmarks bar. If you use another browser, click the "Change Browser" link below and choose Internet Explorer, Firefox, or Safari from the drop-down menu and follow their own specific installation instructions.

How to use the Sharing Bookmarklet

1. Find interesting articles online.

2. Click on "share on LinkedIn" from your browser toolbar.

3. Add a comment to put your own spin on the item you are posting.

4. Choose who you want to share it with, and post.

How to Craft Killer LinkedIn Connection Invites in Three Simple Steps

Invite **Nicholas** to connect on LinkedIn

How do you know Nicholas?

- Colleague
- Classmate
- We've done business together
- ● Friend
- Other
- I don't know Nicholas

Include a personal note: (optional)

Hi Nicholas,

I noticed that we were both in the SEO Masters group on LinkedIn, and I'd love to connect to learn more about your work on SEO for blogs, and how we could work together in future.

Are you free for a quick Skype call this Wednesday at 10am?

Kind regards,

[your name]

Important: Only invite people you know well and who know you. Find out why.

Send Invitation or Cancel

Above: An example of an effective connection invite on LinkedIn.

Much of what we have focused on so far relies on doing everything you can to help people find you on LinkedIn, but being pro-active in making connections can bring just as many - if not more - benefits.

If you're serious about connecting with people on LinkedIn (instead of just arbitrarily trying to increase the number of connections you have), you should never, ever use the boilerplate invite: *"I'd like to add you to my professional network on LinkedIn,"* even if it's someone you know. The default message is lazy, impersonal, and unlikely to endear you to anybody that you send it to. Instead, follow these three steps to plan and craft invites and connections that will help you grow a deep and close-knit network.

1. Do your research
If you were applying for a job and preparing for an interview, you wouldn't turn up without having done a little research into the company in question, would you? The same principles hold true for making a connection with someone on LinkedIn. Before you click "Connect," take a look at their profile and understand as much as you can about them - who they are, where they work, what they do, what their interests are, etc.

2. Note commonalities
After you have soaked up as much about a potential connection as possible, make a mental note of at least a couple of things the two of you have in common, whether that be a mutual connection, being part of the same LinkedIn Group (there's more on Groups coming in a later chapter), or interested in a similar area of research.

3. Write a personalized invitation
Finally, it's time to make that connection! Combine the information you have acquired above to pen a short invitation that is going to be memorable, and gives a reason why you want to connect, whether it be for an

opportunity to collaborate or ask if there is a chance that they can offer you some work. Always tailor your message to the individual. An example might read:

Hi Nicholas,

I noticed that we were both in the SEO Masters group on LinkedIn, and I'd love to connect to learn more about your work on SEO for blogs, and how we could work together in future.

Are you free for a quick Skype call this Wednesday at 10am?.

Kind regards,

[your name]

People like to deal with people they feel like they can trust, so spending a short time to make your invites personal can really make the difference between a great new connection and fresh opportunities coming your way, or a *lost* opportunity and your message being dismissed without a second's thought.

How to Encourage Quality Recommendations: Priceless Testimonials From Colleagues and Friends

Mark Roberge
SVP of Sales and Services at HubSpot

❝ I subscribe to 100+ blogs on sales best practices but only two of them are forwarded directly to my email. Greg's blog is one of them. I sincerely appreciate the predictable, analytical, and process-oriented approach Greg and his team take to sales strategy. Following his blog is like a daily dose of a top notch sales lecture.

June 22, 2011, Mark was a consultant or contractor to Greg at Sales Benchmark Index

Above: An example of a typical LinkedIn Recommendation

One way to help boost your chances as a job-seeker on LinkedIn is to gather testimonials - or Recommendations as they are known on LinkedIn. Ideally, these would come from former colleagues or satisfied. Research suggests that LinkedIn users whose profiles contain recommendations are three times as likely to get inquiries through LinkedIn searches. And, of course, you can use the recommendations you receive to promote yourself on your website and other marketing materials too.

Why get recommended?
- It helps you hire and get hired
- It helps you find customers and partners
- It builds your brand and reputation
- It makes your network more valuable

Who should recommend you?

- Former managers
- Colleagues and co-workers
- Customers and clients
- Business partners

How to ask for recommendations

Asking contacts, ex-colleagues, ex-clients, and even current clients for recommendations is very simple to do.

1. Hover over the "Profile" link at the top of your LinkedIn profile and choose "Recommendations" from the drop-down menu. On the next page, you'll land on a tab to manage the recommendations you have received.
2. Here, click "Ask to be recommended" next to any of the positions listed or click the "Ask for recommendations" tab.
3. Choose what position you want to be recommended for, who you want to ask (type the names or click the address book icon to find them that way), and create a message to send to them. The default message reads as follows, but you'll want to customize it to get the most people interested as possible.:

"I'm sending this to ask you for a brief recommendation of my work that I can include in my LinkedIn profile. If you have any questions, let me know.

Thanks in advance for helping me out.

[Your name].

4. When you're done, hit Send.

To maximize your success rate, ask for recommendations from people you have recently worked with or connected to.

Group your recommendation requests
While you can add up to 200 recipients at a time when asking for recommendations, I would suggest you ask several groups of people on different days instead, perhaps spread over a couple of weeks. Not only will this allow you to somewhat personalize the message you send - no one likes a default one - but it will also prevent your profile from being swamped by recommendations over a very short period of time, which might look a little suspicious to anyone in your extended LinkedIn network potentially eyeing you up.

Delete the default message and add something specific to the group of people you're asking. Ask politely if they'd be willing to post a recommendation in regard to the value of your work while you are/were colleagues together .

Manage your recommendations
Right underneath each position on the "Received" recommendations tab, you'll see a link where you can click to manage the praise that has been left for you. Click that and you'll be shown a list of the recommendations given to you for that particular role. From here you can "request a new or revised recommendation" - although you have to remember that they might not be as enthusiastic second time around, especially if you're asking them to change it considerably!

This page also allows you to check or uncheck the "show" boxes next to each recommendation. This will determine whether they are visible on your profile or not. If you only have a few weak recommendations from friends and family - which might do more harm than good - you might want to hide them until you get a few really positive ones instead.

Don't feel compelled to return the favor... at least not immediately

The best recommendations are those that appear without you having to ask for them in the first place. If someone is kind enough to leave you some positive words after you asked, don't immediately feel that you have to leave them a recommendation in return - even if LinkedIn prompts you to do so. "Recommendation swaps" have the peculiar effect of diminishing the value of both gestures, no matter how genuine. This isn't to say you shouldn't eve return the favor to someone who has given you a recommendation - it's good manners after all - but don't feel forced into it immediately.

How to move recommendations from one job to another

One last thing work mentioning about recommendations is that you can move them from one job experience to another, although the process is neither quick nor easy if you have lots of them. To move a recommendation, you must delete the position that the recommendations are listed under. Once they become unassigned recommendations, you can assign them to a different job position.

How to Use LinkedIn Groups to Grow Your Connections And Become An Authority Figure In Your Profession

Above: Inviting a LinkedIn Group member to connect

LinkedIn has a huge and thriving community of Groups on its site, and they provide a perfect place for you to get to share your expertise, get to know people, and earn connections - both given and received.

How to find and join Groups
You can find and join LinkedIn Groups from the Groups Directory or the Groups You May Like pages, both available by hovering on the "Groups" link at the top of your LinkedIn profile. To join a Group, click "Join Group" on the group's Discussions page or anywhere you see the button.

How to connect with people in Groups

You can find new people to connect with by looking through a Group's active discussions or by viewing the list of Groups that your desired connection belongs to. Request to join said group, engage with them, and then ask connect by hovering over their profile image within the group and choosing the "Invite to connect" link. When you belong to the same group as someone and go to connect with them, just select the "Groups" when asked how you know that member.

Best practice dictates that you have at least engaged with an individual in a group before sending them a custom invitation. The last thing you want is for them to mark your invite as spam and contribute to you having your ability to connect restricted!

How to start discussions in LinkedIn Groups to grow exposure and authority
LinkedIn allows you to start discussions with your Groups too - just type in the box at the top of a group, including links if you wish. You can use this option to drive traffic back to content you have created on your website and your blog, but the real bonus here is that sharing content with relevant groups can turn from exposure just within your Groups to upwards of thousands of LinkedIn members if it is "Liked" or commented on.

By contributing regularly to LinkedIn Groups you have joined, or managing one of your own, over time you will increase your reputation is an individual who is knowledgeable and well-versed in your field, and this will encourage people to want to connect with you for future opportunities.

Currently Unemployed? What to Put in Your Headline, Summary, and Current Position Sections

If you're unemployed, the question of what to list in your LinkedIn profile's Headline, Summary, and Current Position can be a bit of a difficult one because, even though you're between jobs, you still want to present yourself in a positive light to prospective employers. First of all, it is best to be honest about your situation, rather than to lie and cause trouble for yourself with a new employer down the line. Assuming you've filled out all of your previous experience and additional sections (education, volunteering, courses, etc.), here are some suggestions:

Mention you are seeking work in your Summary section

As well as including all of the key information in your Summary section mentioned earlier in this book, include the fact that you are open to new opportunities or looking for more work.

Post a status update mentioning that you're looking for work

If you have recently been laid off, it is a good idea to update your LinkedIn status to alert your network that you are looking for a job. Maybe they can pass the word on and help find you a new position. One example might read: *"Joshua is interested in freelance opportunities. Let him know if someone in your network needs help with web design and coding."*

Be open in your Headline
As your Headline is so prominent and important SEO-wise to your LinkedIn profile, even if you are unemployed you should fill it in, particularly with keywords that you think your next potential employer will be looking for. Unemployed LinkedIn Headline examples include:

- *Unemployed and Looking for Work*
- *Expert Marketing Manager Seeking Work*
- *Experienced Personal Trainer available for new opportunity*
- *Neuroscience professional in transition*
- *Financial Advisor currently exploring options*
- *Recent College Graduate Seeking Entry Level HR Position*

... And the same goes for yoyr Current Position
Listing your current position when unemployed can be tough too. I've seen many Profiles that list "Unemployed" or "Seeking New Position" as the company name. Another option, if you're doing freelance or consulting work is to list your company as self-employed. Unemployed LinkedIn Current Position examples include:

- *Open to Opportunities at Seeking New Position*
- *Looking for a job in Advertising at Unemployed*
- *Student at College.edu*
- *Recent Graduate at College.edu*
- *Consultant at Self-Employed*
- *Seeking a Position at Unemployed*

- *Unemployed and looking for a great job at Unemployed*
- *Freelance Writer at Self-Employed*

As you can see, filling in these key sections of your LinkedIn profile when unemployed involves making the most of what you've got, and doing the most you can to make yourself visible to recruiters and prospects within search.

How to Find A New Job on LinkedIn (And How to Keep Your Search Secret From Your Current Employer!)

Above: Searching for a job on LinkedIn

How to search for jobs on LinkedIn

LinkedIn makes it easy for users to search for available job listings on the site. To begin, visit http://www.linkedin.com/job/home or click the "Jobs" link at the top of the site. Here, you'll be presented with a search bar to look for jobs by title, keywords or company name. And if you click the "Advanced Search" link, you can filter the search by country, Industry, Zip Code, Functions, (and if you're a Premium member) by Salary too. Below, you'll also see recommended job listings based on the details provided in your LinkedIn profile.

Above: Adjusting your LinkedIn Privacy settings.

How to keep your LinkedIn job search a secret from your current employer

It may be the case that you want to use LinkedIn to search for a new job, but don't want to alert your current employer (who might be connected to you on LinkedIn) for obvious reasons. Making new connections, when you haven't been previously, could alert your employer to your impending departure before you really want to. Luckily, you can adjust your Privacy Settings to prevent this from happening. Here's how:

1. Hover over your name on the upper-right side of your profile, and click on "Settings."

2. Under the Privacy Controls menu on the next page, click on the "Turn on/off your activity broadcasts" link.
3. Un-check the box that says "Let people know when you change your profile, make recommendations, or follow companies." Save changes.
4. Click on "Select Who Can See Your Activity Feed" link. From the drop-down menu, choose "Only You. Save changes.
5. While you are in your Account Settings, make sure the e-mail address you use is a personal one. If it's a company one and you leave, the first thing that will happen is that your company e-mail address will be removed and you might have difficulty accessing your LinkedIn account thereafter.

Other ways to keep your LinkedIn job search secret

- Don't post that you are in a job search in your status updates or on your profile.
- Edit your profile and uncheck the box that you are open to career opportunities.
- Don't post in LinkedIn Groups that you are looking for a new job.

LinkedIn Premium Memberships: What Are They And Are They Worth The Money?

LinkedIn offers a variety premium accounts for those people looking to get the very most of everything the site has to offer, and they are particularly geared towards recruiters, job seekers, sales professionals, and individuals with different needs. To view them, click on the "Upgrade" link at the top of your LinkedIn profile.

For the majority of people, LinkedIn free features are sufficient enough. However, if you are keen to try the pro features, you can select to sign up for just a month to see if you like the benefits it brings. Here is an overview of the different premium accounts available:

LinkedIn Premium Business Plus

- Plans start at $10.95 per month
- See who has viewed your profile
- See full profiles of people you are not connected to
- Send direct messages to anyone on LinkedIn regardless of connection
- Get more introductions
- Let anyone message you
- Gain access to premium search filters
- See more profiles in search results
- Create saved search alerts
- Get a full list of people who can provide a reference for someone you are interested in.

LinkedIn Premium Talent Finder

- Plans start at $39.95 per month
- See who has viewed your profile
- Give you full network visibility regardless of connection
- Send direct messages to anyone
- Use premium search filters.

LinkedIn Job Seeker Premium

- Plans start at $19.95
- Allow you to send direct messages regardless of connection
- Be a featured applicant when applying to jobs on LinkedIn
- Get a premium badge so you stand out in search results when recruiters are looking to hire
- See who has viewed your profile

- Get access to a job seeker group and webinar.

LinkedIn Sales Navigator
- Plans start at $15.95 per
- Get sales alerts
- Gain access to a lead builder to manage your pipeline
- Pinpoint leads with premium search filters
- See full profiles
- See who has viewed your profile
- Get introductions
- Send direct messages to anyone regardless of connection.

How to Export Your LinkedIn Profile to PDF to Save it from Lost Data Mishaps

Above: Exporting your LinkedIn profile to PDF

Have you ever lost an important piece of digital work because you didn't back up a copy of it elsewhere? I know I have, and it's a horrible, stomach-jerking feeling! After putting so much work into your LinkedIn profile, you should take a moment to back it up too as, like any website, LinkedIn could at one point in time be vulnerable to data losses no matter how secure they claim to be. If a time ever came that your profile did somehow disappear, at least you'd have all of the information at hand to populate a new one without too much effort.

How to make a PDF back up of your LinkedIn Profile

On your Profile page, click the little arrow next to the "Edit Profile" button and choose "Export to PDF" from the drop-down menu. Your LinkedIn profile will instantly be downloaded and saved as a PDF.

Note: You'll need the free Adobe PDF reader to export your profile. If you haven't got it, grab it here: http://get.adobe.com/uk/reader/

As a heads-up, the PDF copy of your LinkedIn profile is a text-only document, so you won't see your profile image or any media samples that you may have included.

Top Online Tools to Manage Your LinkedIn Profile and Analyze Its Effectiveness

If you want a more streamlined method of managing your LinkedIn activity, and get lots of additional insights about your LinkedIn activity beyond what LinkedIn offers, there are plenty of tools to help you do so. They're not free, but if you're super serious about optimizing your LinkedIn strategy, then they might be worth the investment:

Oktopost (http://www.oktopost.com/):
Schedule status updates to your LinkedIn profile and groups, and get statistics about how many clicks you receive on your status updates from your profile and LinkedIn groups.

Jumplead (http://www.jumplead.com/)
Analyze visitors coming to your website via LinkedIn, and manage your LinkedIn leads.

HootSuite (http://hootsuite.com/) Publish and schedule status updates to your LinkedIn profile and other popular social networks

Buffer (http://bufferapp.com/)
Schedule status updates for your Twitter, Facebook, and LinkedIn profile.

I Need You: Help Make This Book Even Better!

Outdated, not-working tips

As hard as I work to keep the content of this book as fresh and up-to-date as possible, small details and technicalities can fall through the cracks. If you try out a tip or instruction and notice that it is out of date, no longer working as it should, please, *please* let me know via the contact details in the "About the Author" section of this book so that I can rectify the issue in the next version.

Typos and grammar

The same as the above goes for typos or grammatical errors. I do my best to weed them out as often as possible, but as the book is updated so frequently, there is always a chance that they will sneak their way in! If you spot any glaring errors that you think need my attention immediately, do get in touch, so I can change them at the first available opportunity. Thank you very much!

Got a tip to share?

If you have a tip that you think deserves a place in any section of this book, then drop me a line via the "About the Author" section. I'd love to feature you and your genius little ideas!

Work With Me! Social Media Design,
Analysis and Management

Since writing *500 Social Media Marketing Tips*, I have been contacted by many businesses who want help with their social media strategy - either from the beginning of their venture, or just for reassurance that they are on the right path. I am pleased to say that I offer a range of tailor-made, affordable one-off services and ongoing packages to help consult on, build and manage social media marketing for your business. My rates are very reasonable and negotiable dependent on your needs and budget. Services offered include:

- Social Media Strategy Audit / Analysis
- Social Media Profile Setup and Design
- Social Profile Management and Audience Building
- Social Media Strategy and Profile Design Analysis And Recommendations

If you would like more information on pricing or would like to get me on board to help you with social media in any way, please visit the 'Work With Me' page at my website, http://www.andrewmacarthy.com or email me on amacarthy85@gmail.com

I look forward to hearing from you!

About the Author

Andrew Macarthy is a blogger and social media strategist from Swansea in Wales, UK. His #1 Web Marketing Kindle Bestseller, 500 Social Media Marketing Tips, helped thousands of businesses with simple, practical advice to optimize their social media activity and make the most of the sector's marketing opportunities.

In his spare time, Andrew enjoys running, Nintendo videogames, acoustic guitar, and Swansea City FC. Read more at andrewmacarthy.com

Any Feedback or Questions?
Email me at amacarthy85@gmail.com or contact me on the following social networks.

Facebook: http://www.facebook.com/500socialmediatips
Twitter: http://www.twitter.com/andrewmacarthy
Pinterest: http://www.pinterest.com/andrewmacarthy
YouTube:
http://www.youtube.com/user/500socialmediatips

One Last Thing...

If you believe the book is worth sharing, please would you take a few seconds to let your friends know about it? If it turns out to make a difference in their lives, they'll be forever grateful to you, as will I.

In addition, if you have a few moments now to leave a short review on the Amazon product page, please, please do. Something that only takes you a few moments will help me out today and for years to come.

All the best, and thank you so much for reading my book.

Andrew.